Tractors

Paul Stickland

MATHEW PRICE LIMITED

The tractor is ploughing the fields ready for sowing.

The seagulls are looking for worms.

The seagulls love this. The plough throws up all the worms near the surface, so they have a good meal.

The plough has eight blades, four in the ground at a time. As the tractor goes across the field, they slice into the earth and then lift and turn the soil ready for sowing.

The SAFETY CAB *is very important on steep hills.*

STEERING
WHEEL

EXHAUST PIPE

Heavy weights are fitted to the front of the tractor to balance the weight of the plough.

ENGINE

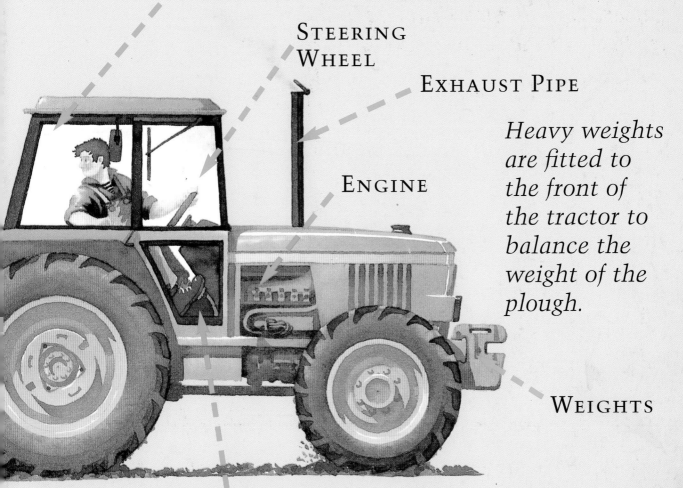

WEIGHTS

ACCELERATOR
PEDAL

The driver has to make sure the field is neatly ploughed. He is looking back to check that his line is straight.

This huge tractor can push
as well as pull.

Sometimes tractors break down
and need to be mended.

This type of tractor is very powerful. It is used for pulling and pushing heavy loads. It can travel quite fast on the road, but not as fast as a car.

HANDLE

to pull yourself up by.

LADDER

to climb up and down.

It has four huge tyres, all the same size. It has four wheel drive for maximum grip: all four wheels are driven by the engine, not just two.

RADIATOR GRILL

Air gets in here to cool the engine.

All machines have to be looked after. Sometimes they go to a garage to be mended, but often the mechanic will have to make repairs in the open field.

BRIGHT LIGHTS for seeing behind you in the dark.

Different attachments and different trailers hitch on to this iron frame.

In this TOOLBOX are all the tools needed to get the tractor working again. There are spanners, wrenches, screwdrivers and of course a hammer. There are also machines to test the electrics. The mechanic will carry replacement parts.

Women drive tractors as well as men.

This old man is taking his sheep to market.

You need to be able to see behind you in a tractor. These large mirrors jut out much more than mirrors on a car, so you can see exactly what is happening.

The exhaust pipe has a flap on top to stop rain getting into the engine.

EXHAUST PIPE

MIRROR

MIRROR

TREADS
Huge treads give traction on a muddy field.

AXLE

The axle joins the wheels to the chassis. It has to be very strong because tractors bump over so much rough ground. There is an axle for the front and one for the back wheels.

This is what tractors looked like fifty years ago. They were smaller and less powerful. Tractors replaced horses on a farm and changed a way of life that had lasted for centuries.

The poor driver had to sit in the open in all weathers because tractors had no cab. Imagine driving out to feed your animals in the pouring rain.

These sheep are going to market to be sold.

People collect old tractors like this. They will be repaired and cleaned up so that they look much better than they did when they were working.

This trailer is full of fresh cut grass going

to the farm to be stored for winter.

The trailer can carry grain and vegetables too.
What else do you think it could carry?

This trailer can carry a load of 10 tons. It can tip up and pour the load out of the back.

TAIL LIGHTS
for going on the highway.

EXTRA WIDE TYRES
These spread the weight of the load. It means that the trailer can be pulled over soft muddy ground.

The main danger for the driver is working along a steep hillside. This cab is strong enough to protect the driver from being crushed if the tractor overturns.

SAFETY CAB

EXHAUST PIPE

It is tall so that the fumes don't go in the cab.

STEPS UP

HEADLIGHTS

Farmers often have to work early in the morning and late at night.

The green tractor has a digger attached to it.

It is loading earth into the red trailer.

Tractors have many attachments.
This front loader is easily fitted to
the heavy metal frame of the chassis.

FRONT LOADER

HYDRAULIC ARMS

PISTONS

TAILGATE

The power for the loader comes from
the tractor's hydraulic system. It is
driven by the engine and pushes the
pistons in and out. The pistons control
the arms and the bucket.

BUCKET

Trailers come in all shapes and sizes. This one has low sides. This allows it to be loaded easily.

MUD FLAPS
to stop mud
spraying up from
the wheels.

As trailers have to carry heavy loads like rocks and earth, they are made of very strong steel. Even so, after years of use, a trailer can get very battered.

The **How, Why, What For** Page

Old tractor: why is this dangerous?

Caterpillar tracks: why do you have these?

What's this for?

New tractor:
what's new?

Extra fat tyres:
why?

What's this for?

The **Answers** Page

Caterpillar tracks can go over ground that is too rocky or slippery even for a tractor's huge treads.

For going over soft ground.

There is no safety cab.

It's a disk harrow, for breaking down clods of earth so the seeds can be evenly sown.

There is a safety cab, wing mirrors and better head-lights. The treads on the tyres are better too.

It's a forage harvester. It picks up cut grass and pours it into a trailer.

Copyright © Paul Stickland 1992, 2004

This edition first published in the UK 2004
by Mathew Price Limited
The Old Glove Factory, Bristol Road
Sherborne, Dorset DT9 4HP, UK

Designed by Douglas Martin
Printed in China
ISBN 1-84248-112-6